PRAISES FOR SHE WINS

Very moving and uplifting! After reading, you will feel encouraged to make things happen for yourself. Andromeda reminds you that you are equipped with the qualities necessary to achieve as much success as you are confident enough to go after.

-CORINE MARIE

EVERY sentence gave me life and reminded me of my WHY! Thank you for this book, I know it will touch many lives. I can't wait to read the entire book. I need a t-shirt that says: I am my own Superhero

- ERICA DIAS

She Wins is a must read for every woman in her life-time. A winning attitude is not optional and She Wins teaches us valuable lessons and key strategies to attain success in life and conquer the fears that far too often hold us captive.

- ARDRE ORIE

It's so empowering and encouraging, and it's said in a way that will make you get up and make it happen. I think it's great. It's going to help and inspire so many women, as you already do.

-SHONDA BROWN WHITE

So powerful and inspirational!

-IKESHIA SMITH

SHE
WINS!

The ultimate guide for women to gain a winning mindset and lead a winning lifestyle.

ANDROMEDA
RAHEEM

Printed in the United States of America

First Printing, 2017

ISBN: 978-0-9985210-3-9

WWW.13THANDJOAN.COM

TABLE OF CONTENTS

FOREWORD

I REMEMBER it like yesterday. It was rigid cold outside, a winter storm was in full effect, and there was literally a sheet of ice that started in our driveway and stretched for at least three to four miles down the main road. What started off as a mild winter storm quickly turned into what some referred to as a major ice storm – particularly for those who live further down south. Hence, it was quite obvious why my husband thought it was crazy that I was willing to take a risk and drive approximately 30 minutes through the so-called treacherous weather.

Although my husband knows how much I love women's empowerment events and vision board parties, and since I had attended so many in the past, he suggested that I sit this one out and wait for the next one. He had a point, because quite honestly I had already completed a vision board, and all of the local news stations were warning people to stay off the roads as much as possible. However, I had waited so long for this moment, and I didn't want to miss it this time around. It was similar to one of those episodes from the hit TV show "Catfish" when they've been waiting forever to finally meet the person they've been talking to forever. The only difference this time was that this person was who they said they were, and they were just as awesome, friendly, and supportive in person as they appeared to be online.

It wasn't until I explained to him how important this was to me, and why I felt the need to push through anyway. "This is different, my love," is what I told him. "I really want to show my support especially since they're in the city. We didn't have a chance to link up the last time they were here." Needless to say, my husband, being the supportive man he is, took one for the team and he drove me to the event. Although it was a slow commute, and at times dangerous, I'm glad to say it was all well worth it because that was the first day I officially met Andromeda in person. When she had each and every one of us go around the room and write down a compliment about every other woman in the room and share it aloud, I told myself, "Yeah, she's the real deal." Only Andromeda could take something that can be so hard for some women, and make it pretty easy for a room full of women who hardly knew each other.

See, that's the type of affect Andromeda has on other people. She gives off such a positive energy, and she makes everyone around her feel important and supported. So, it's quite naturally you want to be around her and support her, and you're encouraged to do the same for someone else. It's no wonder that she has a following of more than seventy-five thousand and a business network that continues to flourish on a daily basis. It's no wonder why she's been invited to speak numerous times across the nation to share her testimony, her story, and her success. She's a natural born leader who encourages positivity and empowerment for all women. I'm proud to say I know her, but I'm even more blessed to call her friend.

I remember a few years ago when I first started following the Women By Choice (WBC) Instagram page, and later started following Andromeda's personal page. Although it has grown significantly since the beginning, the same is still true - no matter the day of the week or the time of day, there is always a quote or a saying that provides just the boost and inspiration I need to live fearlessly, and to embrace the God-given power living within me. The fact that her movement encouraged us, as women, to truly support each other really attracted me to Andromeda and WBC. Nowadays, it's pretty easy to find similar pages or other women who talk about women empowerment and supporting each other, but Andromeda actually means it and lives it.

I've witnessed Andromeda's supportive spirit since day one when we first connected via social media. I will never forget how much she supported me, in more ways than one, during the release of my second book. It's easy for others to cheer for you when everyone else is cheering for you, but it means even that much more when someone ends up being one of the first to do it. The fact that Andromeda supported me without first meeting me face to face, and despite the fact that I wasn't even an official member of WBC yet spoke volumes. To be acknowledged by a woman like Andromeda - someone with a huge following, who has women admiring and following her from all around the world – and to know that she connected with my book was one of the best compliments and one of the greatest highlights for me that year. It's no wonder that our relationship has grown beyond a business relationship, and it's obvious there's a greater reason why we connected in the first place like we did. Simply put, real recognizes real.

Trust me, if you had told me some years ago that I would develop new friendships and relationships via social media, I wouldn't have believed it, but now I do. I remember when Andromeda spoke about struggling to find genuine, authentic, and loyal friends. I could totally relate, because I have also struggled with that throughout my life especially when it comes to making "new friends." Thankfully, however, I've never been concerned with that since the first day we met.

When you're committed to living on purpose and living out your dreams, it's critical to connect with people who understand you; people who understand the highs and the lows, the peaks and the valleys. When I text or call Andromeda, I know I can be myself with her. She gets me, she gets it, and we get each other. We don't have to talk every single day, but when we do you know it's going to be powerful and encouraging even if it's only for a few moments. We can be real with each other even on those days when it can be a bit discouraging, or when your mind is playing tricks and trying to convince you to give up. Like Andromeda, I wear many hats, and sometimes you give so much of yourself to everyone else that it becomes easy to forget about yourself. So, on those days when we need a little encouragement, we're there for each other as fellow wives, fellow women empowerment mavens and authors, and more importantly as sisters supporting each other.

What I love most about Andromeda is the fact that she really means it when she says, "When women support women, we all win." Her story, her social media following, as well as her network of awesome, talented, and powerful women through the WBC network is a testament to that, and a testament to what a positive and supportive network of women can do and produce. It wasn't too long ago that I met even more amazing women who are committed to her movement at local events and even in other cities...all because of Andromeda. She truly exemplifies what it means to not have to dim someone else's light just so your light can shine too. We can all shine together. I'm in awe at the mere fact that I have the distinct and honorable pleasure of writing this foreword at this very moment, knowing that I get to shine the light on someone who has shined it for so long for so many other women.

Andromeda isn't just the founder and leader of WBC. She isn't just the woman you see on your social media timelines. She is every woman. She is your sister. She's been where we've been more than we may even realize. She understands what it means to be a woman. She's the one who will tell you to keep running when you want to stop. She's the one who will tell you to dust yourself off and keep it moving. She's the one who will tell you to stop whining and start winning!

Andromeda truly wants each and every one of us to win. Because she's winning and has helped me and thousands of other women win too, she knows and understands what it takes to be victorious. She's lived through it, and she's learned because of it. She knows how to overcome obstacles and maneuver through detours no matter what life throws at her. So, who better to learn from and be inspired by than someone like her? I hope you're ready to win, because Andromeda is ready to ignite the flame within you. She is an empowered woman who will empower you even more as you will soon see through her words in this book. I'm excited and confident that my sister will motivate you to win, and I hope you're ready to join Andromeda in the winner's circle!

— SHONDA BROWN WHITE

Acknowledgements

For my father who has always told me
that I am destined to win and my mother
who has always supported me to win.

An open letter to women who win

GREETINGS WINNING WOMAN,

I am here to tell you no matter who you are or where you've been, you can win. After experiencing years of revolving doors of friendship and unhealthy interactions with females, I decided to turn my pain into power and walk in my purpose of uniting and empowering women. I believe that it was necessary for me to have those discouraging experiences so that I could show women how to overcome negativity and become better instead of bitter. You see, there was a time in my life when I built a wall around my heart to keep all females out because I was so tired of the drama, cattiness, betrayal, and lack of support. I was completely over it. That was until I chose to let go of the anger I had been carrying and I realized that building a wall didn't make me stop wanting genuine friendships with women I could grow with. It was then that I chose to break down that wall and stop punishing all women and myself for the few that disappointed me. Choosing to become better instead of staying bitter was one of the best choices of my life. That choice lead me down a remarkable path to creating a global network for women and connecting with some of the most amazing women on the planet. I say all of that to say, no matter what happened in the past or what obstacles you may face in the future, you are still in the game. You can still choose to win.

I wrote this book to encourage and empower all women to tap into the best versions of themselves and push themselves to reach their full potential. I believe that when we learn, we must teach each other. Women uniting and supporting each other to win is so important because whether we want to admit it or not, we need each other and we are stronger together. Individually we are powerful, but together we are unstoppable. Plus, winning is way more fun when you can celebrate your wins with other women.

The hard truth is that we are all living in the same world and if the world does not improve then we will all suffer. We are much more connected than we may realize. Everything that we do or don't do affects someone else. It's vital that we respect one another and genuinely care about each other's well-being. A woman who is happy, healthy, confident and successful will have better interactions with the people around her, including her children and family. The impact of our choices can last for generations. Even though it may not appear to affect you when you see another woman in your community struggling, one day her children may negatively affect your children because they did not grow up in a healthy environment. We are our sister's keepers. We have the power to stop negative cycles and end generational curses.

Winning looks like different things to different women, but ultimately a woman who wins is a woman who lives a life that meets her own definition of happiness and success. A winning woman is a woman who is confident in her choices, empowered to succeed, and satisfied with the direction her life is headed in. To live a winning life-style, you must be motivated, disciplined, faithful, resil-ient, and determined to get everything that your heart desires. You must know that you were created for great-ness and abundance and be courageous enough to go after it. I wasn't always the empowered woman I am today. To become the woman I am today, I had to step out of my comfort zone, face my fears, quit running from difficulty, and make myself accountable for making my dreams a reality. It was a journey and I am still learning daily, but I want to share what I have learned to assist other women to win. When women support women, we all win!

ONE:

SHE
WINS

Think Like
A Winner

ONE:

SHE WINS BECAUSE SHE KNOWS THAT SHE CAN.

WAS RAISED to believe that I can do anything that I set my mind to. Growing up, my father always told me that winning is my destiny. I learned early on that winning begins with your mindset. Although there will always be outside forces that can slow you down, once you know your worth and understand the power you have, there will be nothing that can stop you from winning. Your thoughts control your actions. If you make up your mind to win then you will.

Before you set out to achieve any goal, you must first believe that you can achieve it. You must be confident in your ability to complete what you start. You must know that you deserve to have what you want. Avoid doubting yourself, questioning if you deserve it, or sabotaging yourself by overthinking everything. If you want something, make a strategic plan and commit to getting it. If you don't know how to do something, don't fret, learn it. If you fall, don't lay in the dirt, get back up. If you fail, don't beat yourself up, try again. You must know that you hold the key to your success and you decide whether you win or lose. This is your life and you are responsible for your choices and the rewards or punishments that come with them. Within you is everything that you need to succeed. With a sound mind and strong-willed heart, you can do anything. You do not need anyone's permission to make your dreams a reality. Winning is your destiny. Trust in yourself and your ability to win. Know that you can do this.

SELF-EVALUATION: On a scale of 1-10 (10 being the highest), how confident are you in your ability to win? What are the contributing factors to your confidence or lack thereof?

I am an unstoppable force. I am powerful beyond measure. I can do anything that I put my mind to. I am worthy of living a life that I love. I deserve to win.

TWO:

SHE WINS BECAUSE WINNING IS HER ONLY OPTION.

WHILE ON THE path to pursuing my goals, I have never lost, I have only learned. When things didn't go as planned, I didn't give up, I took what I learned and created a new plan. Once you make up your mind to win, winning becomes the only option. Everything you want and everything you dream of having is attainable. It's all a matter of how far and for how long you are willing to go to get to it. To win, you must lose the option to quit. As soon as you make up your mind to do something, consider it done. Don't stop until you get it. Plan A is to win. Plan B is to refer to Plan A.

It is important to understand that it is normal to experience obstacles and challenges when striving for greater. In pursuit of your goals, when things become more difficult that does not always mean that you should run for the nearest exit. Often times, discomfort is a sign that you are growing. When women experience childbirth, they go through a series of changes and pains leading up to the birth of their blessing. Your journey to reaching your goals is similar. When you start feeling more discomfort and pressure, it doesn't mean that you are losing, it means that you are rising to a new level and getting closer to your breakthrough. Embrace your journey for what it is even when it's painful. "No pain, no gain." Trust the process and keep taking steps forward. Avoid focusing on how far away you are or how long it will take to reach the finish line. Instead, focus on taking one step at a time. Each step will get you closer to where you're trying to go. Before you know it, you will be right where you planned to be.

MOMENT OF REFLECTION: Think of a time when you set a goal and quit before you reached it. Do you have any regrets? Think of a time when you set a goal and pursued it until you achieved it. What happened next?

When you are on the road to doing good things, achieving your dreams, and reaching your goals, you will run into traffic, speed bumps, and roadblocks. It may force you to slow down, but don't go back and never give up.

THREE:

She Wins because she guards her thoughts and watches her words.

YOUR THOUGHTS are powerful. They shape the reality you live in. Once I came to that realization, I became more conscious of my thoughts and who and what I allow to influence them. I only allow myself to entertain thoughts that will lead me to win.

Life looks different to different people simply because everyone has different perspectives. Your thoughts have the power to manifest things into your life because your thoughts guide your words and actions. Your thoughts have the power to give you peace or cause you to be immersed in chaos. A woman with an optimistic mind, who looks for the positives in every situation and chooses to maintain a positive attitude is intentionally manifesting a positive life for herself. A woman who always thinks negatively, looks for negativity, and dwells on negativity is manifesting her own personal hell.

Check yourself and do some soul searching when you find yourself thinking negatively. If you know that the words that are about to come off your lips aren't coming from a place of positivity, it's probably best that you keep them to yourself. Once you speak them, you can't unsay them. The energy you exude is the energy you will attract so don't send it out if you won't be happy to get it back. Be intentional about your thoughts and words because every action has a consequence. Monitor your thoughts regularly to ensure that you aren't becoming your own worst enemy. Think twice before you speak and only say what you wouldn't mind repeated.

SELF-CHECK: Are you more prone to seeking out the positives or dwelling on the negatives? Are the things that you read, listen to, and surround yourself with encouraging you to have positive or negative thoughts?

Reserve space in your mind for only the things that make you better, happier, and wealthier.

FOUR

SHE WINS BECAUSE SHE DOESN'T TAKE EVERYTHING PERSONALLY.

FOUND SO MUCH more time to be productive and happy once I stopped taking everything that other people do personally. I learned that other people only have power over me when I give them the power to steal my time and affect my energy. The only person that you can control is you. You are going to spend a lot of days miserable if you waste much of your time and energy being upset because of what other people say and do. You cannot control other people, but you can control who you allow around you and your reactions to the people around you.

Every minute you waste upset is a minute you could be using to progress. Before you allow yourself to spend a significant amount of time being bothered by the actions of others, actions you can not control, ask yourself if it is really worth it. Are they worth the time you could be spending smiling and enjoying life? Are they worth the energy you could be using to improve yourself or complete tasks on your to-do list? How people treat you says much more about them than it does about you. Think about that before you react and entertain nonsense. What do you want your reaction to say about you? Choose to rise above negativity and avoid allowing the actions of others to get the best of you. Life is short and there is much to do. Use your time and energy wisely.

SELF-CHECK: How much time do you spend a week complaining and worrying about the actions of others? What could you be doing instead that would be more productive?

Power is accepting that you can't control other people and deciding that you won't allow them to control you either.

FIVE:

SHE WINS BECAUSE SHE IS NOBODY'S VICTIM.

YOU ALWAYS HAVE the choice to be a victim or survivor. You can choose to allow bad experiences to break you or make you stronger. You can choose to allow others to write your story for you or you can take back the pen and choose how your story ends.

Life won't always seem fair. Not everyone will support your endeavors. People will hurt and disappoint you. Things won't always go as you plan. Sometimes you will fail at your first, second, and third attempts. However, spare yourself the pity parties. It is a waste of time to sulk in disappointment, doubt, and discouragement. No good will come from it. The time you spend complaining and dwelling over your problems is the same time that you could be using to heal from your pain and find solutions to your problems. The harsh reality is that you can't depend on anyone to come and save you and you can't count on other people to feel sorry enough for you to help you. You must be willing to save yourself and seek out the help that you need. You must find the strength within to pull it together even when you feel like falling apart because your goals don't care how you feel. Choose to take control of your emotions and use them to motivate you to push harder and rise higher. Choose to turn your pain into power by taking what you learned through your experiences and flip the negatives into positives. Choose not to be a victim of your trials, but a survivor of your struggles.

SELF-CHECK: Do you feel like a victim in any area of your life? What steps can you take to reclaim your power?

Today, I am in a great mood. I am overflowing with joy. My heart is strong, my body is healthy, and my mind is at peace. I have abundant energy and my thoughts are full of positivity. I am blessed with supportive friends and family. I represent class, grace, and beauty. I know my worth and my confidence level is high. Today, I am winning.

THOUGHTS

....

....

....

....

....

....

....

....

....

....

....

....

....

....

....

....

....

TWO:
WORK & WIN

ONE:

SHE WINS BECAUSE SHE WORKS FOR WHAT SHE WANTS.

I HATE TO BE the one to break it to you, but dreams don't come true by wishing on stars and problems aren't solved by complaining on your couch. The level you reach in life is directly related to the amount of effort you put in. You can either work for what you want or wait for what you want, but just know that if you choose to wait, you may never get what you want.

Speak it, plan it, then do it. Visions become a reality with effort and action. If you want it, you are going to have to work for it. There is no way around it. Whether it be getting to the altar, dropping some unwanted pounds, or earning a specific income, you will have to invest time and exert energy. Speak what you want to see happen daily. Write down your goals and research the steps you need to take to reach them. Then, create a strategic plan and put it into action. To win, you must be intentional with your time and strategic with your moves. You must be committed to using all of your gifts, talents, and abilities.

Women who win choose to work smart by learning all that they can. Read and research. Learn from those who have already been where you are trying to go. The more knowledge you have, the more power you have, and the easier it will be to achieve your desired results. Winning has a great deal to do with what you know and how you manage your time. Everyone has the same 24 hours, but successful people choose to use their time more wisely than others. Time is your most precious asset. Once it's gone, you can't get it back. If you are willing to sacrifice more of the time you spend being entertained to learn something, you will find yourself spending more time living the life that you want.

SELF-CHECK: Does the effort you put in match the lifestyle you want to live? If not, what can you do differently?

She doesn't get what she wants because she wishes and waits. She gets what she wants because she works and prays.

TWO

SHE WINS BECAUSE SHE IS DISCIPLINED AND CONSISTENT.

A **MAJOR SHIFT** occurred in my life the moment I decided to get disciplined and consistent. The results that I had been waiting years to see happened in months once I became disciplined with how I spend my time and consistent with performing positive and effective actions. What separates the winners from the losers is discipline and consistency. Discipline is what winners have and losers lack. Consistency is a major key to achieving any goal you set out to reach.

Having discipline allows you to channel your energy in exactly the areas you want to see improvement in instead of being all over the place, completing nothing, and making no progress. By having a clear idea of what you aim to achieve and placing yourself on a schedule that will enforce effective action, you can guarantee that you will win. No matter what the goal is, if you consistently work towards achieving it, it is only a matter of time before you reach your desired destination. By continuously repeating effective actions, you can guarantee progress. Think of yourself walking down a long road with your destination too far in the distance to see clearly. Even when you can't tell that you are making progress, you know that you are with each step that you take forward. Whether it be a health or a wealth goal, it's your discipline to stay focused and consistent steps forward that will lead to your success. Create an effective plan of action and discipline yourself to follow through with it. You can either demand yourself to do what you know you need to do to achieve your goals or you can fly by the seat of your pants and see where you land. The quality of your life is based on your decisions. Make choices that will guarantee wins.

SELF-CHECK: What area(s) of your life do you think would improve if you were more disciplined and consistent?

I know my worth and will not be satisfied with nor accept anything less than what I deserve. My time is valuable and I will not waste it on things that do not serve a positive purpose. I am in charge of my health, wealth, happiness, and success. I choose to use my energy to win.

THREE:

SHE WINS BECAUSE SHE DOESN'T PROCRASTINATE.

FOR MOST OF my life, one of my greatest weaknesses was procrastination. I never really saw it as a weakness though because I considered myself a person who works well under pressure. If I had a deadline, I would reach it even if I waited until the last minute. However, I came to realize that operating in that manner was causing me unnecessary stress and robbing me of time. I learned that I was doing myself a major disservice by waiting to do things that I had the time to do sooner.

Time waits for no woman. Don't put off for tomorrow what you can do today because you have no idea what challenges tomorrow will bring. The only moment you have for sure is the current one you are in. It is much better to be ahead of the game than to get behind because you waited. If you can do it now then get it done. By staying ahead, you free up time to do more of what you want without the constant reminder that there is something you need to do. By completing tasks ahead of schedule, you allow yourself more room to create more goals and achieve them in less time.

You can't complain about your progress if you aren't giving your 100% to the process. Use your time wisely.

Don't make excuses not to do what you know you need to do to live the life that you want to live. It's not rocket science, you get what you give. If you wait to do it later then be prepared to receive it later. The longer you take to get started, the longer it will take for you to get there. The sooner you get started, the closer you will be to finishing. The hardest part is taking that first step. Push yourself to take it even when you don't feel like it. Do what you need to do so that you can live how you want to.

MOMENT OF REFLECTION: What have you been wanting to do, but waiting to do?

Don't let procrastination stop your progress. There is no time to waste, you have a beautiful life to create.

FOUR:

SHE WINS BECAUSE SHE IS HER OWN SUPERHERO.

ONE OF THE greatest lessons I have learned in my lifetime is that this world won't give me anything for free. Although winning is my destiny, I had to come to the understanding that I am not entitled to success. I must earn it. If you want something, you must be willing to do what it takes to get it. Whatever you want to see happen in your life, you have to be brave and determined enough to make it happen. You can't sit around waiting for a man or anyone else to come and save you. You can't wait for someone else to see the potential in you. You have to be willing to be your own superhero. Don't be afraid to ask for what you want and then go after it. When need be, create your own opportunities.

You may not always have the amount of support that you think you need to succeed, but as long as you are determined to proceed without it, you will win. The people you start your journey with may not be the same people you finish with. As you are rising, not everyone will be able to rise with you. People will come and people will go so you must always be prepared to do what you need to do to achieve your goals, even when that means working alone. Your life is your responsibility. You have to live with the results of what you do and what you don't do. Blaming other people for your lack of achievements or progression is a waste of time. It won't help to move you forward. Have greater expectations of yourself than you do of other people and you will spend far less days discouraged and disappointed. Be open to asking for and receiving help, but decide not to be held back due to lack of it. Choose to make yourself accountable for securing your own winning position.

MOMENT OF REFLECTION: What is your superpower? What makes you great?

I am a woman who is not bound by the chains of the thoughts and opinions of others. I do not need approval from others to create a life I love. I walk boldly and fiercely in my purpose. I choose to win.

THOUGHTS

....
....
....
....
....
....
....
....
....
....
....
....
....
....
....
....
....

THREE

WINNING WITHOUT COMPETING

ONE:

SHE WINS BECAUSE SHE RUNS HER OWN RACE.

IN LIFE, IT can be difficult not to look over to see how far and fast others are going on their journeys. However, winning is not about competing with someone else's pace, winning is about measuring your own progress on the way to your desired destination. The only person you are truly in competition with is yourself. You are in competition with the woman you were yesterday. You are in competition with the weakest parts of your mind and body. You are competing with yourself to become strong enough to overcome the pains of your past and your bad habits. You have plenty of things to compete with all by yourself. Work on you before seeking out competition anywhere else.

The world is full of distractions, influences, and people that can steer you in a direction you don't want to go in, if you allow it. Determine your purpose and what you want to achieve in this life then get focused. Create your own lane and run your own race. It is pointless to compete with others when you are walking different paths and have been dealt different hands. You are the only person in your life who is fully aware of your reality and the internal and external battles you are fighting daily. Your only competition is yourself. The goal should not be to defeat others, but to defeat your weaknesses and reach your full potential. If your goal is to improve daily then you are already winning.

REVIEW: Who are you in competition with?

She silently stepped out of the race that she never wanted to be in, found her own lane, and proceeded to win.

TWO:

SHE WINS BECAUSE SHE DOESN'T COMPARE HERSELF TO OTHERS.

STOPPED COMPARING myself to other women once I came to understand that comparing my life to someone else's is like comparing apples and oranges. There is not another soul walking this Earth who has walked in the same shoes, on the same path, and at the same time as me. My journey is unique and can never be fairly compared.

Although you have access to view highlights of other people's lives, do not get so caught up in what you see others doing that you begin to form comparisons. Comparing yourself to others can cause loss of joy, encourage feelings of jealousy, and decrease confidence. You can never fairly compare yourself to others because your journey is like none other. You were not meant to be the same as everyone else. You were created for a particular purpose. Your goals and dreams won't match the goals and dreams of everyone you meet. You won't be attracted to every trend you see. It's not necessary for you to alter who you are to fit in. Embrace who you are and your reality. Make the most of where you are and what you have. Do the best you can with the cards you have been dealt. Count your own blessings. Define your own success. Live up to your own definition of happiness. What works for one may not work for you, but what's meant for you will always be for you.

SELF-CHECK: Do you find yourself comparing yourself to others? Why? How does it make you feel?

She never compares herself to other women because her goals and values may be different.

THREE:

SHE WINS BECAUSE SHE IS FOCUSED ON IMPROVING HERSELF, NOT ON IMPRESSING OTHERS.

THE GOAL SHOULD not be to become who others want you to be, it should be to become the best possible version of yourself. If you are always trying to impress others, you are thinking more about who they would like you to be than becoming who you were created to be. The thing about being an impressive individual is that people will notice that you are impressive without you having to tell them. A genius doesn't have to tell anyone that they're a genius, it will show in their actions and their lifestyle.

It is better to use your time and energy to achieve permanent greatness than to receive temporary attention. A woman who leaves a legacy is a woman who spent her life improving herself daily. Winning is not about impressing and competing with others, it's about proving to yourself what you are capable of. You don't need to try to prove to people that you're worthy. Work in a way that your worth speaks for itself. A great way to lose yourself and sight of your purpose is by trying to please everyone else or convince others that your life is good. Simply live a good life and to others it will be obvious. You will never win if you are always trying to "keep up with the Joneses" because you will always be running behind someone else in their lane. Find your own path and define your own happiness and success. You will find that once you become truly happy with yourself and where you are in life, the validation of others will become less important. The more confident you are in yourself and your choices, the less you will live for the approval of others.

SELF-CHECK: Do you find yourself worrying about others opinions before you make life decisions? What impact do their opinions have on your ability to win?

A winning woman lives her life in a way that is best for her mentally, physically, emotionally, and financially. She focuses on improving herself instead of impressing others.

FOUR:

SHE WINS BECAUSE SHE DOESN'T TRY TO FIT INTO EVERY CIRCLE.

LOOKING BACK, I spent too much of my life trying to fit into circles that I never belonged in. I spent way too much time trying to convince people who could never understand me that I was worthy of their attention. There is a certain amount of power that comes once you understand that you are not meant for everyone and not everyone is meant for you. There is a certain amount of confidence that comes once you realize that you wouldn't be as special if you fit into every circle.

Imagine the world as a puzzle and each person being a puzzle piece. We all have a place where we fit perfectly without force. When we all are in the right position and serving our purpose, we make a beautiful picture. A life spent trying to cut and paste to fit in is a life that is extremely limited. You can never become your best self trying to be something other than yourself. Trying to get every person you meet to like you is like you going into the grocery store and liking every product on the shelf. You won't be liked and appreciated everywhere that you go and that is okay. Accept that fact then find the courage to be who you are. Of the billions of people in the world, there are many people who will love you exactly as you are. You don't need to change who you are to try to meet everyone's expectations. You only need to be true to yourself so that the people who were created to love and appreciate you can find you. Your soul mate and best friends won't be able to identify you if you look, sound, and act like someone completely different. Be brave enough to be yourself so that you won't have to spend your whole life feeling like you are by yourself.

SELF-CHECK: Are you in circles where you are appreciated or tolerated? Do you fit just right or are you forcing it?

She wins because she understands that her calling isn't for everybody. She focuses on quality, not quantity.

THOUGHTS

....

....

....

....

....

....

....

....

....

....

....

....

....

....

....

....

FOUR:

FAITH + WORKS = WINNING

ONE:

SHE WINS BECAUSE SHE PREPARES FOR WHAT SHE PRAYS FOR.

I AM A HEAVY praying woman, but I learned that I can pray as much as I want and it won't do me any good if my prayers aren't followed up with actions that match. Praying, but not working will hinder your progress. Whether you are praying for a house or a husband, you have to prepare to receive what you desire. You must have faith and be willing to do the work to win.

Pray for what you desire then create a plan for how you will get to a position that aligns with your prayers. Once you create your plan, take steps daily to execute it. Nothing is just going to fall out of the sky and into your lap. You can't receive opportunities if you're not in the right place at the right time for them to be presented to you. I'm not encouraging gambling, but you can't win the lottery if you don't play the lottery. Your husband won't find you if you're not showing up in your life. You can't reap a harvest if you haven't sown any seeds. Blessings aren't just given, they are earned. What's for you is for you, but you have to be willing to do your part to receive it. Get on your knees and pray then get on your feet and work.

SELF-CHECK: Do your prayers match your actions or are you moving in the opposite direction of what you are praying for?

Today, I realize my power and my strength. I will do everything I set my mind to do. I will be a woman of my word. I will walk with grace and confidence. I will show the world who I am and prove to myself what I am made of. I will be true to myself without fear of criticism or rejection. Today, I will win.

SHE WINS BECAUSE SHE IS PATIENT WITH HER PROGRESS AND TRUSTS THE PROCESS.

WINNING IS A journey, not a destination. If you do it right, you'll be winning your entire life. Patience is a requirement to win. Without it, I found my emotions going up and down between excitement and discouragement. When my achievements occurred quickly, I was excited. When they were few and far between, I was discouraged. That was until I learned that throughout the course of my life, I will experience different seasons. Some seasons will be a time to reap and some will be a time to sow. In every season, whether it looks like it or not, you are experiencing growth.

The process will be far less painful if you understand it and choose to trust it. You can't plant a seed today and expect it to be fully blossomed tomorrow. There are certain stages of growth that a plant must go through before it blooms and the same goes for you. Instead of trying to rush to the finish line, be patient with your progress and enjoy the ride. Avoid trying to skip lessons and taking shortcuts that lead to dead ends. Understand that each level of your life will require you to learn a lesson before you can advance to the next level. Set your goals, make your plans, do the work, and patiently wait for the seeds you have planted to grow. To occupy your time while you wait, plant more seeds and take time to celebrate both your small and large accomplishments. The more work you put in and gratitude you have, the more abundant your harvest will be.

SELF-CHECK: Are you enjoying your life or are you rushing your life?

She doesn't beg, force, or chase. She prays, works, and has faith.

THREE:

SHE WINS BECAUSE SHE ISN'T AFRAID TO LOSE.

IF YOU'RE ALWAYS thinking about how embarrassed you'll be if you fail or how disappointed you'll feel if you lose then you will never do what it takes to win. Your faith must be greater than your fear in order to go places you have never been. You must believe in yourself and have faith that good work will yield good results. Your comfort zone may feel safe and secure, but nothing more will grow there. If you want more, you are going to have to be willing to invest more and do more of the things that make you uncomfortable. Don't allow the fear of losing stop you from even trying. Very few people achieve the success they desire because very few people are willing to push through their fears and discomfort to reach their breakthrough. Fear will keep you from greatness if you let it. Faith is believing that there is a net to catch you even when you can't see it. If you lose you can try again, but if you never try, you will never win.

MOMENT OF REFLECTION: What goals aren't you actively pursuing because you are afraid? What is the worst that could happen? Is the risk worth the potential reward?

I push my limits daily so that my future
self will thank me.

FOUR:

SHE WINS BECAUSE SHE DOES NOT LET THE PAST DETERMINE HER FUTURE.

CAN EMPOWER OTHER women to win not because I haven't made any mistakes, but because I have made plenty and learned from them. I could not be the woman that I am today without my past experiences. What gives me the strength to keep going is my faith that everything that I experience happens for a reason. I choose to find the lessons in even my most painful memories.

Everyone has made mistakes, done things that they weren't proud of, and/or experienced situations that they regret. The past happened and there is no magic wand to erase it or time machine to go back and change it. All that you have is today, this moment, right now. Your past only influences your present and future as much as you want it to. Instead of allowing your past to burden you, you can choose to have faith that there is a reason for why you went through what you went through. Ask yourself what you learned from it. Reflect on what you gained from it. Determine how you can use it for your benefit.

The past is where you've been, but not who you are. You don't have to let it to hold you back from who you can become. You can decide in this very moment how your life will be going forward. Your past has already been written, but there are an infinite number of possibilities for your future. Instead of allowing your past to be an excuse for not living the life you want to live, use it as a reference so that you do not repeat the same mistakes again. Make the best of the knowledge you've gained from where you've been and use it to get to where you want to be. Your past does not define you, you define you. Accept the past for what it was and have faith in the possibilities of the future. Who you were doesn't get to determine your future, it's who you are now that gets to decide what you will do next.

MOMENT OF REFLECTION: Think back over your past. Are there any experiences that are negatively impacting the quality of your life? What did you learn from those experiences?

Let your mistakes and life experiences teach and guide you, not define you.

THOUGHTS

....
....
....
....
....
....
....
....
....
....
....
....
....
....
....
....
....

FIVE:
WORK
WITHIN

ONE:

SHE WINS BECAUSE SHE THROWS GLITTER INSTEAD OF SHADE.

IN LIFE, YOU get what you give. It is important to always be mindful of how you treat other people and conscious of the energy you exude. To win, it was necessary for me to stop focusing so much on how other people were treating me and focus more on how I treated others. I found that the more support I gave, the more support I received. The more my actions positively impacted others, the more positive changes I experienced. Being of service to others is a gift that never stops giving.

If you believe that you will reap what you sow then you should understand that you can never lose by assisting others to win. You should also understand that you will never win if you are engaging in behaviors and activities that cause others to lose. If you find pleasure in other people's pain, check yourself. If other people's joy makes you jealous, check yourself. If bringing other people misery makes you happy, check yourself. If you feel negatively about positivity, check yourself. When you're unhappy with yourself, it can be difficult to be happy for others. When things seem like they're not going right in your life, it can be hard to see things going right for others. However, just because you have those feelings doesn't mean that you have to act on them. Your issues and insecurities should not become other people's problem. Instead of allowing your emotions to wreak havoc on your life and the lives of those around you, you can choose to deal with them by determining where they are stemming from. Self-improvement is essential to success. Understand that trying to bring others down to your level will never bring you up to theirs. You won't gain success by being envious. You won't find love in hate. You can't stand in the sun while throwing shade. Give what you want to receive. Treat others how you desire to be treated.

SELF-CHECK: Do you treat other people how you want to be treated?

If you can't stand to see another woman glow up, it's time to grow up.

SHE WINS BECAUSE SHE IS NOT HELD BACK BY HER INSECURITIES.

I USED TO BE insecure about my body so I started going to the gym and eating healthier. I used to be insecure about my level of success so I created a plan and worked to reach a level I could be confident on. I had feelings of insecurity when I decided to write this book, but I wrote it anyway.

You're not weak or abnormal because you have insecurities. Humans are imperfect so it is natural to feel insecure about some things. It's not something to beat yourself up over, but it is something to be aware of to ensure that you're not being controlled by it. Having insecurities can lead to feelings of jealousy and envy. They can cause you to abandon your goals and sabotage your success. Choose not to let your insecurities lead you down a road you will later regret. Use your head. Think your actions through before you make them. Don't allow temporary emotions to cause you to make permanent decisions you will later be unhappy with. Your goals should have priority over your feelings. If you have a clear vision, don't muddy it with irrational emotions. Work through your feelings, control your emotions, and proceed to your desired destination. Avoid being your own worst enemy. Let no one, including yourself, stop you from winning.

SELF-CHECK: On a scale of 1-10 (10 being the highest), how much do your insecurities get in the way of you achieving your goals?

Don't be negative and then wonder why your garden is full of weeds. Plant positive seeds and you will manifest positive things.

THREE

SHE WINS BECAUSE SHE DOESN'T HOLD GRUDGES.

YOU CAN'T GRAB your trophy if your hands are full of the grudges you've been carrying. You have to let what's weighing you down go if you want to win. While you think you're holding a grudge, that grudge is actually holding you. It's holding you back from walking in your purpose and reaching your full potential. If I never dropped the grudge I was holding over all women because of the few that hurt and betrayed me, I would not be successfully walking in my purpose of empowering and uniting women.

Avoid hoarding pain and anger. Forgive people, not for them, but for you. You can't think as clearly and make the best decisions when your heart and mind are harboring grudges. Do not give anyone the power to determine how your story ends just because they contributed to one chapter. If you are carrying any feelings that are holding you back from becoming your best self and reaching your goals, let them go. Release anything that is not beneficial to your health, happiness, and success. Forgive people even when you haven't received an apology so that you can stop allowing them to affect your energy. You have no control over what people do, but you can always choose how you react to them. Choose to love yourself too much to allow the actions of others to bring you down. Instead, rise above them and show them what it looks like to win.

SELF-CHECK: Are you holding grudges? If so, how is it affecting you? Is it worth holding onto?

I release my attachment to anything that is keeping me from being happy. I am done carrying old baggage from past relationships. I am more focused on where I'm going than where I've been. I am too determined to attract positivity to carry hate in my heart for anybody. I am going to win.

FOUR:

SHE WINS BECAUSE SHE SUR-ROUNDS HERSELF WITH WINNERS.

THE PEOPLE YOU surround yourself with and the conversations you contribute to have a great impact on whether you win or lose. The people you associate with should be like-minded in the sense that they are going in a similar direction or have reached a level you are striving to reach. The people around you have the power to influence your thoughts, words, and behaviors. Be sure that the people you surround yourself with are thinking thoughts, speaking words, and performing actions that will influence, inspire, and encourage you to be your best. No one has the power to hold you back without your permission. Give yourself the freedom to grow out of relationships that are no longer providing the energy and inspiration that you need to stay focused and succeed. Your circle can be increased or decreased as needed. In with the winners and out with the people who would be okay with you being a loser.

SELF-CHECK: Do you surround yourself with people who motivate you to think bigger and encourage you to rise higher?

I am not intimidated by strong women, I join forces with them.

I cannot print text by it ???
??? works, ??? not be with them.

FIVE

SHE WINS BECAUSE SHE IS CONFIDENT.

CONFIDENT WOMEN understand that collaborating with other women is more beneficial than competing with them. Confidence allows you to create connections with women who are winning instead of being intimidated by them. Confident women don't have an issue with celebrating the accomplishments of other women. Confidence is a quality that will allow you to shine with other women instead of spending time trying to fight for the spotlight.

The most powerful thing that you can ever do is love yourself. Everything that you do and don't do stems from how you feel about yourself. When you are happy with yourself, it is easy to be happy for others. When you see value in yourself, you can easily find value in others. Confidence gives you the clarity to see that you can build yourself up without knocking other women down. Confidence is necessary to win.

MOMENT OF REFLECTION: What do you love about yourself? What do others love about you? What have you accomplished?

I love myself. I am confident in my own light. I am not threatened by the power I see in other women. Together, we can shine bright.

THOUGHTS

....
....
....
....
....
....
....
....
....
....
....
....
....
....
....
....

A WOMAN'S GUIDE TO

TURNING LOSSES INTO WINS

I: Loss of Friendship
II: Loss of Romantic Relationship
III: Loss of Income
IV: Loss of Opportunity

IN A WORLD WHERE many are suffering in silence because it appears that everyone is winning and very few want to admit that they experience losses, it was necessary for me to write this guide to assist women through their struggles and motivate them to push toward their breakthroughs.

In this guide, you will find words of encouragement to change your frown into a smile and real life tips to turn your pain into power.

LOSS OF FRIENDSHIP

One thing that life has taught me is that every person you meet comes into your life for a reason, even if just for a season. Your friendships, no matter how short or how long, are all meant to teach you something. I had a friend that taught me how to be a good friend simply because she was a bad one. I had a friend who taught me what it feels like to end friendships, without providing a reason, the day she stopped communicating with me without expressing why. This is something I had done to others in the past so when it was done to me, I learned how terrible it feels and decided that I would never end a friendship in that manner again. I had a friend who taught me how to say "no" and showed me that it was okay to make my happiness a priority after I got tired of giving more than I was receiving in that friendship. I had a friend who taught me how to be a better communicator by refusing to discuss our issues via text message, something I had a habit of doing because I didn't like confrontation. Although ending some friendships hurt my heart more than others, being able to see what I learned from them made the separation easier to get over.

Ending a friendship can be painful, especially when it's one that you have had for a significant length of time. However, you can turn your pain into power by accepting that growth is a part of life. As you are learning more about yourself and growing into the woman you were created to be so are the women around you. Two people who start down a road together may not reach the end of the road together because at some point, one may start moving faster than the other or one may slow down. One may choose to change their direction while the other is committed to the road they are traveling. It is natural to outgrow people. Not everyone can go where you are going and not everyone wants to. Allow yourself the freedom to grow without guilt and give others the same courtesy. You do not belong to anyone and no one belongs to you. We were all born to fulfill our own destinies. Sometimes that means being a lifelong friend to someone and sometimes that means being a friend for a few seasons. If a friendship is holding you back or moving you in the wrong direction, you won't be able to keep it. When friendships end sooner than you expect them to, have peace in knowing that it was for a good reason. The best thing that you can do is learn from the experience. That is how you win.

LOSS OF ROMANTIC RELATIONSHIP

One of the most painful moments women experience in life is watching someone we love walk away or walking away from someone we love. Although I have been with the same man for the last 13 years and have been married to him for the last 3, I have experienced heartbreak. As my husband and I were only 17 years old when we first started dating, we experienced plenty of growing pains, heartache, and breakups. Hence the reason why it took us 5 years to get engaged and another 5 to get married. Even as a married couple, during one year of our marriage, I had a moment when I felt like I lost my husband because of the strain that was being put on our relationship due to financial hardship. Over the last 13 years we have lost and found love over and over again. Every time we've been faced with a situation that threatened to tear us apart, but we managed to stay together, we became stronger and learned to value each other more. Our relationship isn't perfect, but it is worth it. It has stood the test of time and I am confident when I say that we are truly meant to be.

When you are truly meant to be with someone, you will know it. You won't need to hold them hostage or have to fight alone to stay together. Much like friendships, there is a purpose behind every relationship that you enter and exit. Some of the most common lessons women learn about failed relationships are:

- Listen to your instincts: Hindsight is always 20/20. You saw the signs and felt deep down that it wouldn't work, but you forced it anyway.

- Not everyone is worthy of your heart: Know your worth and set your standards. You can eliminate a lot of headaches and heartache by not settling for less than you deserve from day one. You know what you have to offer so be clear about what the other person is bringing to the table and be real with yourself about whether or not you can accept it.

- Take the time to heal and improve yourself: Many women jump from one relationship to the next because they crave companionship. If you can relate, the problem with this is that you are likely carrying baggage from past relationships, which is causing you to sabotage yourself and the new relationship. It is necessary that you heal from your pain and become whole again before beginning a new relationship. It is not fair to you or the person you are dating to start a relationship broken and angry. The next man should not have to pay for the pain the previous guy caused you. If you cannot see him for who he is, and not who every other man was, you are not ready to begin a new relationship. Build your relationship on the best possible foundation and you will be strong enough to endure the storms when they come.

Much like loss of friendships, you can turn your frown into a smile by learning the lesson the relationship taught you and becoming a better woman and future wife because of it. Evaluate who you were in the relationship and what attracted you to the relationship. Determine what part (if any) you played in causing it to end. Think about the qualities of the person you were involved with and if you still want to be with a person with the same characteristics. Think about the kind of men you typically attract and are attracted to and determine if there is anything that you need to improve to attract the ideal man for you. You find peace in the ending by understanding that if it is meant to be then the relationship will find a new beginning, but if not, something better is waiting for you. You turn your pain into power by not giving up on love, but by being wiser about who you choose to love.

LOSS OF INCOME

One of the biggest causes for stress is financial difficulties. When you feel stressed about not having enough money to fulfill your financial obligations, it can make it difficult to focus and find solutions to your financial problems. Trust me, I know. I have been there and done that. The year of my life when I felt like I lost my husband due to financial hardships was the toughest year of my life. We got there because, with my husband's blessing, I decided to quit my full-time accounting job to pursue my purpose. We mapped the whole thing out and determined that even if I was not making any money with my business, my husband's income could still cover all of our expenses and then some. Well, that was until he was laid off from his job shortly after we exhausted most of our savings to relocate to a new city. Talk about stressed. Lord knows that if you want to test my faith, shake up my finances. I am naturally one of those people who require financial stability to be happy. I am an emotional mess when my finances are a mess so during a period of that time, I was depressed and had random screaming and crying fits. So, how did I turn that loss into a win? Well, I didn't go run back to my 9-5 or steal or kill to survive. I prayed hard and pushed harder. I learned that in life, you get what you give. Sitting around eating, screaming, and crying wasn't going to change my situation and the longer I stayed in that state, the more hopeless I became. I could not see my way out of the situation until I started to take steps to move myself out of that situation. I took all the energy that I had and put it into my business. There was no more time for excuses because I no longer had the luxury to procrastinate. I gave it all that I had and the result was going from making nothing to having days where I earned $600.00 in just a few hours.

LOSS OF OPPORTUNITY

One thing that life has definitely taught me is that it goes on. Opportunities come and opportunities go. When one door closes, another opens. When I worked a government job, I would get disappointed when I didn't get the promotion I applied for and felt like I deserved. As an entrepreneur, I would get upset when an opportunity that I thought was in perfect alignment with my business wasn't granted to me. That was until I realized that just because I want the opportunity or because I think that it's a perfect fit or perfect timing doesn't mean that it is. If you find yourself dwelling in self-pity when doors close in your face, I encourage you to stop allowing things that you can't control get the best of you. That door may have closed, but if you pay close attention, you will see that another door opened or will be opening. If you do good work and are a good person, then you must trust that things are always working out for your good and likely better than you can even imagine. Thinking back over all the times I thought I lost an opportunity, I can see that behind that perceived loss was a divine win. You will never miss or lose anything that is meant for you. Do your best and trust the timing of your life and you will experience far less discouragement and stress. Do good, be good, and have faith that things, no matter how they look, are working out for your own good.

THOUGHTS

....
....
....
....
....
....
....
....
....
....
....
....
....
....
....
....

Conclusion

TO **WIN IS TO BE** empowered. To be empowered is to change your life. To change your life is to change the world.

I challenge you to empower yourself beyond the pages of this book. There are 3 simple steps to discovering the empowerment of a lifetime. I started the Women By Choice Network because there was dire need for women to support each other to win.

WOMEN BY CHOICE is a network for professional and entrepreneurial women to bring together their collective knowledge and resources to assist each other with reaching common goals. We provide an online and offline environment for women to receive support and information, experience sisterhood, and achieve success through events, education, advertising, and networking. We believe that when women support women, we all win and we are on a mission to break down barriers and bring women together.

HERE ARE 3 EASY WAYS TO GET CONNECTED

Subscribe to our email list at womenbychoice.com to stay updated on the latest events and hottest empowerment products for women.

Follow us on Instagram and Facebook for daily inspiration and motivation.

Join the sisterhood at womenbychoice.com.

About the Author

ANDROMEDA RAHEEM is an Empowerment Coach to women who, in 2014, made the choice to become the change she wants to see in the world. Frustrated with the lack of unity and support among women, Andromeda founded Women By Choice Global, a global network for success-minded women created to break barriers and encourage women to work and win together.

Within 2 years, Andromeda successfully grew a global network for women and a social media platform with an audience of over 100,000 women. Motivated by her passion to see women empowered, united, and winning, Andromeda continues on her mission to break down barriers and bring women together through events, inspirational messages, motivational speaking, business and empowerment coaching, and thought-provoking blogging.

Andromeda's powerful message of "When Women Support Women, We ALL Win" has positively impacted the relationships of women worldwide.

CPSIA information can be obtained
at www.ICGtesting.com
Printed in the USA
FSHW011900190720
71901FS

9 780998 521039